THE **SCIENCE** OF **HISTORY**

T0034233

SCIENCE ON THE
TITANIC

by Tammy Enz

CAPSTONE PRESS
a capstone imprint

Published by Capstone Press, an imprint of Capstone
1710 Roe Crest Drive, North Mankato, Minnesota 56003
capstonepub.com

Copyright © 2023 by Capstone. All rights reserved. No part of this publication may be reproduced in whole or in part, or stored in a retrieval system, or transmitted in any form or by any means, electronic, mechanical, photocopying, recording, or otherwise, without written permission of the publisher.

Library of Congress Cataloging-in-Publication Data is available on the Library of Congress website.
ISBN: 9781666334838 (hardcover)
ISBN: 9781666334845 (paperback)
ISBN: 9781666334852 (ebook PDF)

Summary: You may know about the sinking of the *Titanic*. But did you know science played a big role in the ship's voyage, disaster, and discovery? Learn all about the ship and the events that led to it sinking. Discover how technology uncovered answers to how this famous ship's voyage ended in disaster.

Editorial Credits
Editor: Erika L. Shores; Designer: Heidi Thompson; Media Researchers: Jo Miller and Pam Mitsakos; Production Specialist: Tori Abraham

Image Credits
Alamy: Pictorial Press Ltd, 21, PA Images, 24, World History Archive, 13; Bridgeman Images: Giancarlo Costa, 15; Getty Images: Heritage Images, 17, Jim_Pintar, 11, John Parrot/Stocktrek Images, 5, 45, Krista Few, 40, Ralph White, 39, Star Tribune, 42, United Archives, 27; Shutterstock: Andrey_Kuzmin, 43, BigDane, 36, Boyan Dimitrov, Cover (bottom), 25, Chris Dale, 19, Dimitrios Karamitros, 18, Everett Collection, 29, 31, 32, 35, Fouad A. Saad, 9, grayjay, 37, KamimiArt (design element), ilightmax84, 7, marfuah, 10, MikhailSh, Cover (top), 1, Nicku, 8, Peter Hermes Furian, 12, Sansanorth, 41, Stanislav-Z, 6, Swen Stroop, 34

All internet sites appearing in back matter were available and accurate when this book was sent to press.

TABLE OF CONTENTS

CHAPTER 1
The Unsinkable Luxury Liner......4

CHAPTER 2
Off She Goes 16

CHAPTER 3
The Collision 22

CHAPTER 4
The *Titanic* Today......................38

GLOSSARY 46

READ MORE..47

INTERNET SITES 47

INDEX 48

ABOUT THE AUTHOR 48

Words in **bold** text are included in the glossary.

THE UNSINKABLE LUXURY LINER

In the early 1900s, people traveled overseas by ship. Airplanes were newly invented, and passenger airlines didn't exist. So engineers worked to build better, safer, and faster ships. By 1912, the British White Star line had built the most advanced ship on the seas—the RMS *Titanic*. The *Titanic* had a huge first-class dining room, four elevators, and a swimming pool. Its second-class rooms were as good as first-class rooms on other ships. Even its third-class rooms were comfortable.

Fact

The *Titanic* was 882.5 feet (269 meters) in length and 175 feet (53 m) in height. It cost $7.5 million to build. Today it would cost about $200 million to build.

The ship's designers bragged that it was unsinkable. *Titanic*'s crew was confident in their ship and its technology. On its first voyage, engineers, electricians, and plumbers traveled along to ensure safe sailing.

But the *Titanic* sank on April 15, 1912, during its first voyage. It was headed to New York City from Southampton, England. Science explains how the unthinkable happened to the unsinkable.

The *Titanic* departed Southampton, England, on April 10, 1912.

The *Titanic* was built in the early days of **steam turbine propulsion**. It was powered by two steam engines. They exhausted steam into a single steam turbine. Steam is water heated to 212 degrees Fahrenheit (100 degrees Celsius). It turns into gas. The gas pushes through the system to spin the turbine blades. The spinning power rotates the ship's propellers. Some of the escaping steam was reused to create more power. This technique was known as turbo-compounding.

Stream Turbine Mechanism

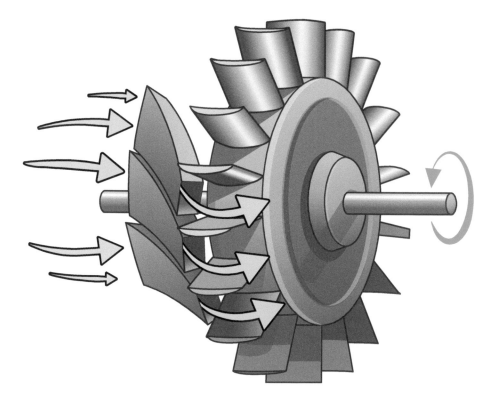

A 176-person crew shoveled coal into the furnaces to boil the water into steam. Each day, the ship burned 825 tons of coal. Every day, 100 tons of ash was pumped into the sea. *Titanic* sailed across the Atlantic Ocean at a speed of 26 miles (42 kilometers) per hour.

Smoke and steam from the engines rose out of three of *Titanic*'s giant smokestacks. Another smokestack was added for looks.

As the *Titanic* sailed across the ocean, steam billowed from three of its four smokestacks.

Fact

The engine of the ship was designed to give 46,000 horsepower. Horsepower is a measure of the power of an engine. It relates to the ability of an actual horse to do work.

Most American homes did not have electricity until the 1930s. In the 1910s, people were still using oil lamps for light. Wood stoves were used for heat and cooking. On the other hand, *Titanic* had electric powered elevators, loudspeakers, heaters, and refrigerators. It also had nearly 10,000 electric light bulbs.

Steam created the ship's electricity by turning the blades of an electrical **generator**. The spinning blades caused an electrical current inside a wire coil. In 1831, Michael Faraday, a British scientist, discovered that spinning a magnet inside a coil of copper wire produced an electrical current in the wire. This is called **electromagnetic induction**. It is how electricity is created today.

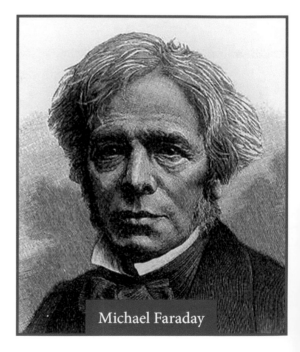

Michael Faraday

The *Titanic* had an electrical control panel 30 to 40 feet (9 to 12 m) long. It controlled all the electrical gadgets onboard. Today a simple laptop or phone could handle the functions of this control panel.

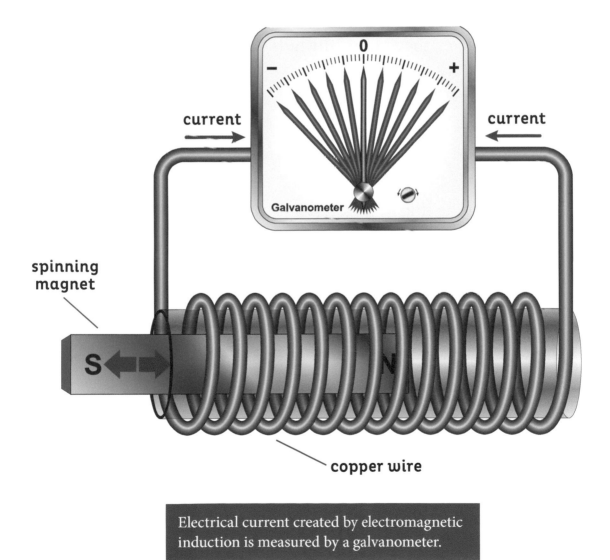

Electrical current created by electromagnetic induction is measured by a galvanometer.

Ships pass through five different time zones when crossing the Atlantic Ocean. There are 24 major time zones.

As Earth spins, the sun sets and rises at different times in different locations. Clocks are adjusted so that 12:00 noon on a clock in each time zone occurs when the sun is directly overhead.

Time Zones

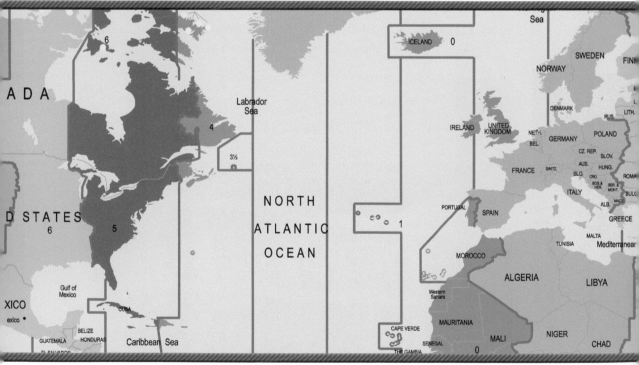

Keeping up with the time zones would mean changing the clocks onboard five times during the trip. But many of the clocks on the *Titanic* were connected to a master clock. The captain could change the time on two master clocks from his command room on the ship's bridge. An electric signal from each master clock would cause the others on board to change.

Nowadays, many digital clocks receive radio signals from an atomic clock in Boulder, Colorado. It keeps the official time in the United States. Radio signals cause the clocks to automatically update when traveling across time zones.

Comfort wasn't the *Titanic*'s only priority. Safety was important. *Titanic* had a state-of-the-art wireless communications system. It sent messages in **Morse code** using radio waves. It could send messages 500 miles (805 km) during the day. At night, messages could be sent even farther. Most ships of the day could only send messages 100 to 150 miles (161 to 241 km) during the day. This system meant the ship could easily send **distress signals** if it needed help.

Radio waves are invisible electromagnetic waves. Electromagnetic waves are all around us. They are created through vibrations in electric and magnetic fields. Visible light is an electromagnetic wave. So are X-rays and radio waves.

Electromagnetic Spectrum

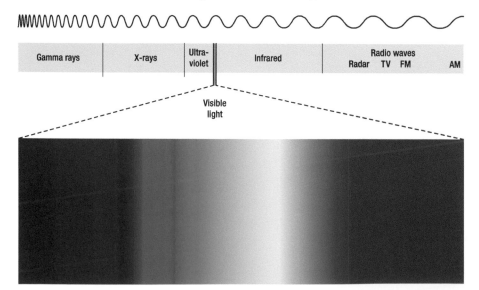

Gamma rays | X-rays | Ultra-violet | Infrared | Radio waves — Radar TV FM | AM

Visible light

Radio waves were sent out through a transmitter on the *Titanic*. They were **decoded** when they reached a receiver far away. Radio waves sent short taps that were decoded into words. Today, radio waves carry music. Cell phones transmit messages on radio waves too.

A man operating a wireless telegraph similar to what was on the *Titanic*

Designers said the ship was unsinkable because it was built with watertight air-filled compartments. Heavy iron ships can only float on water because they are buoyant. Buoyant things weigh less than water. The steel *Titanic* was made from was heavier than water. But the ship floated because it was filled with air. Air is lighter than water.

But if the ship were filled with water, it would sink. So the engineers designed it with 16 compartments. The compartments had doors that could be closed from the bridge. If the hull was damaged, water could be contained in just a few compartments. The rest would hold air to keep the ship floating. The ship's builders claimed that *Titanic* would still float if four of the compartments were flooded. The system led many to claim that the *Titanic* was unsinkable.

Fact
Titanic weighed over 52,000 tons when fully loaded.

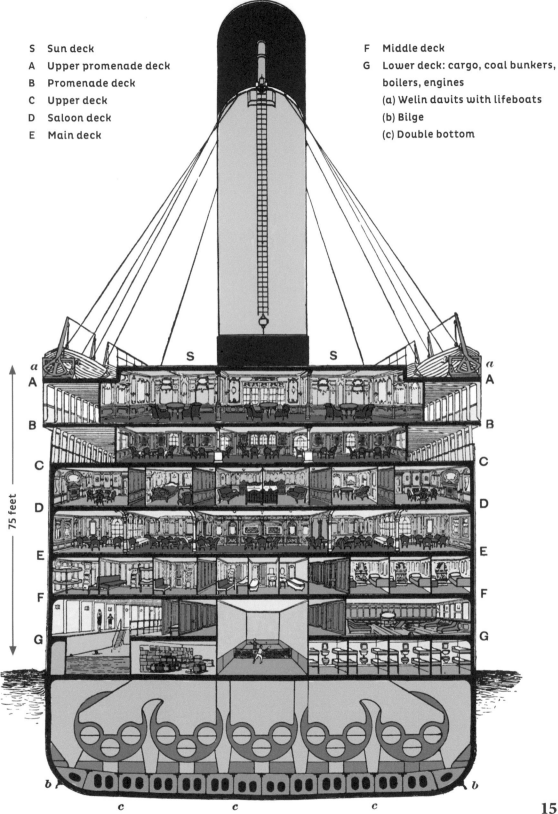

S   Sun deck
A   Upper promenade deck
B   Promenade deck
C   Upper deck
D   Saloon deck
E   Main deck

F   Middle deck
G   Lower deck: cargo, coal bunkers,
    boilers, engines
    (a) Welin davits with lifeboats
    (b) Bilge
    (c) Double bottom

75 feet

S   S

a   a
A   A
B   B
C   C
D   D
E   E
F   F
G   G
b   b
c   c   c

15

CHAPTER 2

OFF SHE GOES

On April 10, 1912, the *Titanic* set sail on its first voyage. The ship's captain was Edward J. Smith.

Right away, the ship's massive size caused problems. It nearly collided with another ship. *Titanic* **suctioned** a docked ship into its path. When a ship moves through the water, it pushes water to the side. If the ship is in a tight space, the water moves faster to squeeze through the tight space. Smaller boats nearby can be pulled into this fast-moving water. It took almost an hour to move away from the other ship.

Titanic made stops in France and Ireland. Again, the size of the ship was a problem. The dock was too small for the *Titanic* to approach. Passengers had to move to and from the ship in smaller boats.

Many of the 1,300 passengers were well-known and rich people. Besides passengers, more than 900 crew members were aboard.

Measuring Speed

The *Titanic* operated at only 21 knots. Knots measure a ship's speed. Sailors in the 1600s measured speed by dropping a log tied to a string with knots at regular intervals. They counted out how many knots rolled out behind the ship in a certain amount of time.

A tugboat helps move a ship away from the *Titanic* as it sets sail.

Long before the *Titanic* set sail, the climate was working against it. Strong winds push ocean water in river-like currents. The Gulf Stream current pushes warm water from Florida along the east coast of the United States.

Another current, the Labrador Current, moves from the Arctic Ocean along the east coast of Canada. It often carries chunks of ice, called icebergs, with it. When the two currents meet, they switch directions. They flow toward Europe, carrying icebergs with them across the Atlantic Ocean.

Gulf Stream and Labrador Current

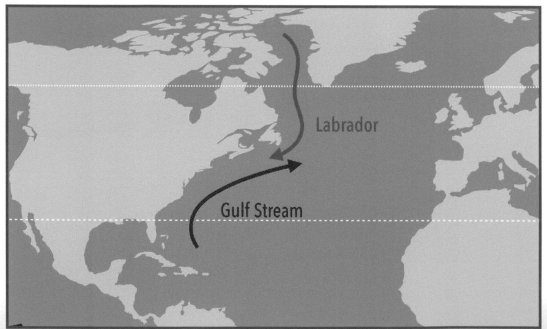

Icebergs are common in the cold northern Atlantic waters.

When weather is warmer than usual in the Caribbean, the Gulf Stream meets the Labrador Current in the North Atlantic. They form an ice barrier. The summer of 1912 was hot in the Caribbean, so the Gulf Stream was intense. *Titanic* was sailing right through the iceberg-filled intersection of the Gulf Stream and the Labrador Current.

The radio operators on *Titanic*, Jack Phillips and Harold Bride, began receiving iceberg warnings early in the trip. They passed the messages along to the bridge. The captain changed the ship's course. He headed farther south to try to avoid the icebergs. But he kept the ship at full speed.

On April 14 at 10:55 p.m., a nearby ship, the *Californian*, sent word that it had stopped. It was surrounded by ice. Phillips was busy handling passenger messages and angrily replied to the *Californian* not to bother him.

Titanic pushed onward toward a huge unseen iceberg. It was between 50 to 100 feet (15 to 30 m) tall. It was 200 to 400 feet (61 to 122 m) long. It was made of a billion tons of frozen water. But most of it was hidden beneath the surface.

The Marconi Company had designed the ship's radio service. The service was popular with *Titanic*'s passengers. In the first 36 hours of the trip, the radio operators sent 250 messages to shore.

CHAPTER 3

THE COLLISION

Lookouts Frederick Fleet and Reginald Lee scanned the ocean for icebergs from the crow's nest of the *Titanic*. A crow's nest is a lookout point on the top of a ship.

Their task was difficult because the ocean was unusually calm that night. The lookouts wouldn't see the waves crashing into an iceberg's base. The lookouts were confused by a "cold air **mirage**," which is relatively common in the North Atlantic.

A cold air mirage happens when warmer air settles on top of colder air. It bends light rays as they move through the changing layers of air. This can cause objects to appear higher in the sky than they actually are.

In the case of the *Titanic*, the horizon would have appeared high in the sky. It would have blended in with the hazy sky. When the lookouts focused on the horizon, they would have missed the iceberg below. This effect may have also prevented nearby ships from seeing the *Titanic*'s warning flares.

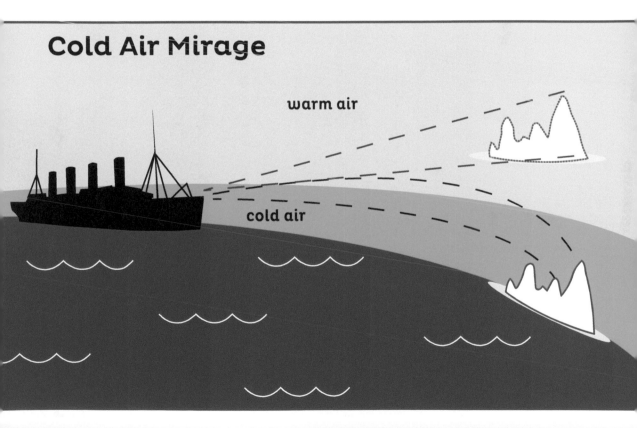

Cold Air Mirage

warm air

cold air

The spotters were supposed to be using binoculars to see better. But *Titanic*'s binoculars were missing.

Around 11:40 p.m., about 400 nautical miles (741 km) south of Newfoundland, Canada, an iceberg suddenly appeared. The lookouts saw it about 37 seconds before the *Titanic* hit it.

First Officer William Murdoch ordered the ship to turn left. He also reversed the engines.

First Officer William Murdoch

The *Titanic* began to turn, but it was too close to avoid collision. The ship's side scraped along the iceberg. Six of its compartments began to fill with water.

Reversing the engines made it difficult to turn the ship quickly. Murdoch's order caused the *Titanic* to turn slower than if it had been moving at its original speed. Most experts believe the ship would have survived if it had hit the iceberg head-on. It would have only ruptured a couple compartments.

Titanic hitting the iceberg

The captain ordered Jack Phillips to send distress signals to other ships. A signal reached nearby *Carpathia* around 12:20 a.m. on April 15. *Carpathia* immediately headed toward the *Titanic*. However, the *Carpathia* was 58 nautical miles (107 km) and more than three hours away. Other ships also responded, but all were too far away. The *Californian* was nearby, but its wireless had been turned off for the night.

The crew began launching lifeboats. Women and children were loaded first. *Titanic*'s 20 boats could carry only 1,178 people. And boats were launched only partly full. Crewmen worried that the davits would not support fully loaded boats. A davit is a long arm, or crane, that extends past a ship's sides. It allows lifeboats to be lowered into the water. Its base is under much stress, especially when it carries a heavy weight at its opposite end.

Fact

The first lifeboat to leave the *Titanic* held only 28 people. It had space for 65.

Davits were used to lower the
lifeboats into the water.

As passengers crowded to enter lifeboats, the ship's musicians played music. Meanwhile *Titanic*'s watertight compartments were failing. The doors had been shut immediately. But there was a design flaw. The compartment walls only extended a few feet above the waterline. As the first few compartments filled with water, they pulled the hull down. Water spilled from one compartment to the next. Air rushed out, and water poured in. The ship lost buoyancy and began to sink.

Some engineers believe that the watertight walls caused the ship to sink faster. If water could have spread out across the bottom of the ship, it would float longer. It could have allowed extra time for nearby ships to arrive to rescue the passengers.

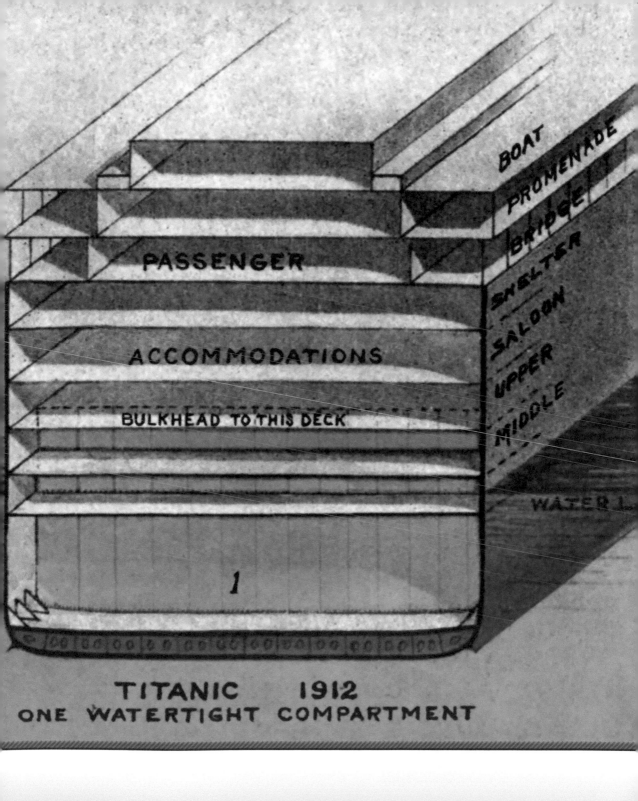

PASSENGER

ACCOMMODATIONS

BULKHEAD TO THIS DECK

1

BOAT

PROMENADE

BRIDGE

SHELTER

SALOON

UPPER

MIDDLE

WATER L

TITANIC 1912
ONE WATERTIGHT COMPARTMENT

By 1:00 a.m. panic set in. People realized the ship would likely sink and there were not enough lifeboats onboard. Phillips's distress calls became desperate.

At about 2:00 a.m. the stern's propellers were visible above the water at the back of the ship. At 2:18 a.m. the lights on the *Titanic* went out.

As the *Titanic*'s front, or bow, continued to sink, the stern rose out of the water. This placed incredible strain on the midsection. The ship was not designed for this stress. It was designed for its weight to be evenly carried by water. It suddenly split in two. The bow sank into the ocean.

The stern settled back in the water before rising again and becoming vertical. It briefly remained in that position before beginning its final plunge. At 2:20 a.m. the stern also disappeared beneath the Atlantic.

Passengers in the lifeboats watched as the *Titanic* sank into the Atlantic.

Passengers who fell into the Atlantic could not survive long in the icy waters.

Hundreds of passengers and crew were dumped into the freezing water. Most had their life jackets on to keep them afloat. But the icy water was dangerous. Its temperature was 28°F (-2°C). The human body needs to stay around 98.6°F (37°C) for all the body systems to work.

The cold water quickly lowered the passengers' body temperatures. When the body temperature drops below 95°F (35°C) **hypothermia** sets in. Hypothermia occurs when the body loses heat faster than it can produce it.

When hypothermia sets in, organs don't work properly. At very low temperatures a person's heart rate and breathing slow down. They eventually stop working, leading to death. People can only survive in these conditions for 15 to 90 minutes.

Fact
The sinking of the *Titanic* took 1,517 lives.

Around 3:30 a.m., the *Carpathia* arrived on the scene and began rescuing survivors. Its crew noticed green light beams shooting from the horizon. These lights, called northern lights or aurora borealis, are caused by solar storms. These sun storms send electrically charged particles toward Earth's **ionosphere**. It is part of Earth's atmosphere that is affected by both the earth's and sun's magnetic fields. The particles become energized, giving off bright colors.

These changes in the magnetic field may have affected the *Titanic*'s compass, altering its route and sending it, unknowingly, toward the icebergs.

An officer on the *Carpathia* said the aurora borealis looked like moonbeams shooting up from the horizon.

Finally around 8:30 a.m. the nearby *Californian* arrived. It had only heard the news three hours earlier. Shortly before 9:00 a.m., the *Carpathia* headed for New York City. It arrived to huge crowds on April 18. The *Carpathia*, led by Arthur Rostron, saved more than 700 lives.

The *Carpathia*

Sadly, if *Titanic*'s lookouts had seen the iceberg sooner, they could have avoided it and changed course. Radar detection technology was still 20 years in the future. Radar can detect icebergs more than 100 miles (161 km) away.

Radar uses radio waves to locate objects and to tell how fast they are moving. Radar can detect objects through clouds and on dark nights.

Radar equipment on top of a modern boat

How Radar Works

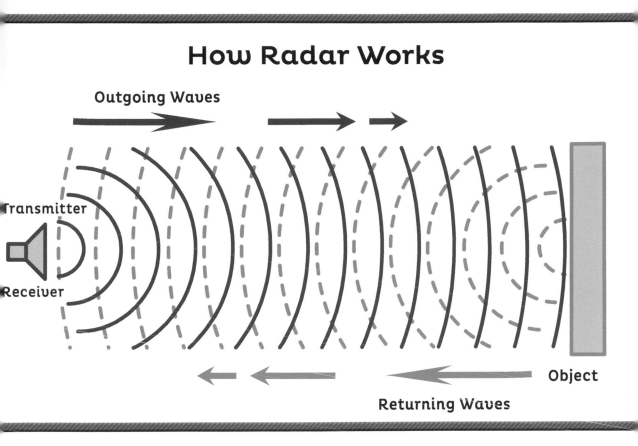

A radar system uses a transmitter to send out radio waves. When those waves hit an object, they bounce back to a receiver. The receiver makes sense of the waves based on how long it takes for them to bounce back. It determines how far away an object is and how fast it is moving.

Fact

After the loss of the *Titanic*, the International Ice Patrol was created in 1914. It tracks icebergs in shipping lanes of the Labrador Current and reports iceberg positions to ships.

THE *TITANIC* TODAY

Soon after the *Titanic*'s sinking, people wanted to find the wreck. But the world had to wait for technology to catch up. In 1985, aboard the U.S. Navy research ship *Knorr*, Robert Ballard finally found the wreck.

Titanic is almost 2.5 miles (4 km) below the surface of the ocean. At this depth, no human diver could survive because of the tremendous water pressure. Normally, air presses on our bodies. This is called air pressure. It presses on our bodies at 14.7 pounds per square inch (101 kilopascals). We don't feel it because the gases in our bodies push outward with the same force. But water pressure is much stronger. Water pressure gets stronger the deeper you go.

At *Titanic*'s resting place, the water pressure would be more than 5,400 pounds per square inch (37,232 kp). At this depth, the water would crush a person. Ballard had to use a pressurized **submersible** sled called *Argo* to reach *Titanic*. *Argo* had cameras to capture what it found. It sent the images back to researchers on the *Knorr*.

Finding *Titanic*

Argo traveled 13,000 feet (3,962 m) to the floor of the Atlantic Ocean. On September 1, 1985, the first underwater images of the *Titanic* were recorded as its giant boilers were discovered. Later video showed the ship lying upright in two pieces.

The *Argo* is prepared for launch.

While the bow was clearly recognizable, the stern section was badly damaged. Rust-colored **stalactite**-like formations covered the wreck. These rusticles were created by iron-eating microorganisms. They are so small that they can't be seen by the human eye. They feed on the hydrogen sulfide produced by corroding iron.

Rusticles hang over the electrical room of the *Titanic*.

Salt water destroys metal as well, through **electrochemical corrosion**. Ions in the salt water attract and dissolve ions on the metal. Ions are electrically charged atoms or molecules. They move toward other ions with opposite charges. This movement of ions from the metal to the water weakens and destroys the metal. Salt water destroys metal five times faster than fresh water.

Scientists continue to explore the wreck. Besides corrosion, deep ocean currents pull and push at the *Titanic*, slowly tearing it apart. By 2019, several walls and other features were completely gone.

Chemicals of Rusting

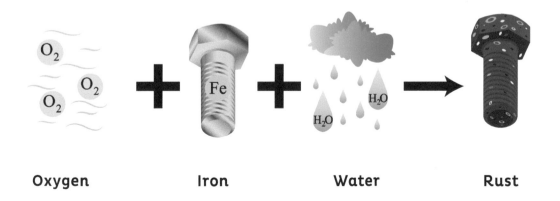

| Oxygen | Iron | Water | Rust |

Expeditions by manned and unmanned submersibles have revealed some interesting finds. Explorers expected to find a long gash on the ship's hull. Instead they found six smaller gashes. They also discovered broken hull plates and separations at the hull seams. These separations would have caused flooding.

A section of the *Titanic*'s hull shows its steel beams.

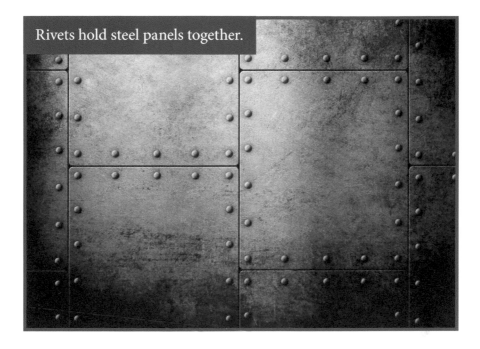
Rivets hold steel panels together.

Poor quality steel and poor construction could have played a role in the fate of the *Titanic*. Scientists noticed that pieces of steel from the *Titanic*'s hull were jagged and sharp like broken glass. It didn't bend or deform like high quality steel. The advantage of building with high quality steel is that it can bend and deform before breaking.

Scientists also noticed that the rivets used to hold the pieces of steel together at the ship's hull were imperfect and not properly inserted. These rivets could have pulled apart more easily during the collision.

Another theory has recently surfaced. Researcher Senan Molony discovered a large black mark on the front of the ship's hull in a photograph taken before it set sail. No one had studied these marks before.

Molony believes that a fire burning at 1,832°F (1,000°C) went unnoticed in the ship's underbelly for weeks. It could have weakened its steel.

Steel is a metal **alloy**. It is made from iron mixed with other metals to make it very strong, yet flexible. It bends and stretches when it changes temperature or when it gets hit. But steel loses its flexibility if it is burned. Some of the metals in the alloy burn up, leaving steel weak. It can lose up to 75 percent of its strength. It is more likely to shatter when hit.

Was it fire or was it ice that sealed *Titanic*'s destiny? We still don't know for sure. The *Titanic* met its end more than 100 years ago. But science continues to play a big part in understanding its final fate.

The steel underside and the propellers of the *Titanic* are visible in this photo taken before the ship's launch.

GLOSSARY

alloy (AL-loy)—a substance made up of two or more metals

decode (dee-KOHD)—to change a code into language we can understand

distress signal (di-STRES SIG-nuhl)—a call for help

electrochemical corrosion (i-lek-troh-CEM-uh-kuhl kuh-ROH-shuhn)—water eating away at metal little by little

electromagnetic induction (i-lek-troh-mag-NET-ik in-DUK-shuhn)—producing an electrical current by changing a magnetic field

generator (JEN-uh-ray-tur)—a machine that makes electricity using the movement of magnets next to coils of wire

hypothermia (hy-po-THER-me-uh)—dangerously low body temperature

ionosphere (EYE-on-oh-sfeer)—part of Earth's upper atmosphere

mirage (muh-RAZH)—something that appears to be there but is not

Morse code (MORSS KODE)—a method of sending messages by radio using a series of long and short clicks

stalactite (stuh-LAK-tite)—a growth that hangs from the ceiling of a cave, formed by dripping water

steam turbine propulsion (STEEM TUR-bine pro-PUHL-shuhn)—forward movement created by a machine with steam-powered blades

submersible (suhb-MURS-uh-buhl)—a small vessel used under water

suction (SUHK-shuhn)—drawing air out of a space to create a vacuum; air or liquid is sucked into the empty space

READ MORE

Freeburg, Jessica. *A Titanic Time Capsule: Artifacts of the Sunken Ship*. North Mankato, MN: Capstone, 2021

Halls, Kelly Milner. *The Mystery of the Titanic: A Historical Investigation for Kids*. Emeryville, CA: Rockridge Press, 2021.

Messner, Kate. *History Smashers: The Titanic*. New York: Random House Children's Books, 2021.

INTERNET SITES

Remembering the Titanic
kids.nationalgeographic.com/history/article/a-titanic-anniversary

Titanic Facts
sciencekids.co.nz/sciencefacts/engineering/titanic.html

Titanic Facts for Kids
kids.kiddle.co/Titanic

INDEX

Argo, 39
aurora borealis, 34

Ballard, Robert, 38, 39
Bride, Harold, 20
bridge, 11, 14, 20

Californian, 20, 26, 35
Carpathia, 26, 34, 35
cold air mirage, 22, 23
collision, 24, 25, 43
compartments, 14, 25, 28
crow's nest, 22

electricity, 8, 9
electrochemical corrosion, 41
electromagnetic induction, 8, 9
electromagnetic waves, 12
engineers, 4, 5, 14
engines, 6, 7, 24, 25

Faraday, Michael, 8
fire, 44
Fleet, Frederick, 22

hull, 14, 28, 42, 43, 44
hypothermia, 33

icebergs, 18, 19, 20, 22, 23, 24, 25,
    34, 36, 37

Knorr, 38, 39

Labrador Current, 18, 19, 37
Lee, Reginald, 22
lifeboats, 26, 27, 28, 30, 31
lookouts, 22, 23, 24

Molony, Senan, 44
Murdoch, William, 24, 25

passengers, 16, 17, 20, 21, 26, 28, 31,
    32, 33, 35
Phillips, Jack, 20, 26, 30

radar, 36, 37
radio operators, 20, 21
radio waves, 12, 13, 36, 37

sinking, 5, 14, 28, 30, 31, 33, 38
size, 4, 14, 16
Smith, Edward J., 16, 20, 26
steam turbine propulsion, 6
submersibles, 39, 42

time zones, 10, 11

water pressure, 38, 39
wireless communications system, 12

ABOUT THE AUTHOR

Tammy Enz holds a bachelor's degree in Civil Engineering and a master's degree in Journalism and Mass Communications. She teaches at the University of Wisconsin-Platteville and has written dozens of books on science and engineering topics for young people.